Preface

The NOF French for 10th grade book is based on the latest curriculum released by National Olympiad Foundation for French language.

The main aim of writing this book is to help students in the preparation for their NOF exam and to give an in-depth knowledge of French language with the aid of languages that they already know. This book serves as a multilingual guide for revision of the NOF syllabus. We have made every effort to make this book as comprehensible as possible for a student with enough questions to get them ready for the exam.

The key features of this book are:

- It provides Hindi and English translations for all the questions and answers, which ensure the correct understanding of every piece of information, and saves time spent on translating words using dictionaries.

- To give a wholesome knowledge of the language every question is accompanied by it's French pronunciation in English and Hindi to improve students' reading and pronunciation along with their understanding.

- The syllabus provided by NOF is divided into three categories: Introduction of France, French culture & civilization and French grammar in order to simplify and arrange the content for students.

The book is therefore your indispensable guide for NOF exam.

Bonne préparation à tous !

Manish Soni
Ashi Goel

Index

1. Introduction of France

La France; L'enseignement; La cuisine française; les goûts; les loisirs et la détente; la santé; le travail; lire et s'informer; les transports en France; les institutions politiques; les apports de la science; l'informatique

2. Grammar

Les articles; les prépositions; les adjectifs démonstratifs; les pronoms démonstratifs; les pronoms possessifs; les adjectifs possessifs; les pronoms interrogatifs; les adjectifs interrogatifs; le présent de l'indicatif; le futur; le conditionnel présent; le conditionnel passe; le passé composé; l'imparfait; le plus-que-parfait; le participe présent; le gérondif; le style direct et indirect; subjonctif; les pronom personnel; les pronoms relatifs composés; l'impératif; le futur antérieur; les proverbes; la forme nominal

3. Culture and civilisation

La Corse; le tour de France; le festival de Cannes; le festival d'Avignon; la carte de France; les fleuves et les reliefs; les villes françaises; la fête de la musique; la fête des mères; la fête des pères; Jacques Prévert; le système d'éducation en France; Université de Paris-Sorbonne; le Crous; les plats francais; les spécialité; le théâtre; le cinéma; les musées; Molière; la sécurité; ANPE; C.V.; Annonces classées; la presse; la bibliothèque; carte de lecteur; la télévision; la Fontaine; Antoine de Saint Exupéry; métro; carte orange; SNCF; TGV; RATP; voitures française; code de la route; le minitel; la télécarte; le système politique en France; le mèl; l'internet; le site web; la publicité

Table of Contents

Chapter 1

1. ___फ्रांस का एक शहर है।

(___ is a French city.)

(___ est une ville française.)

(___ए त्युन वील फ्रौंसैज़।)

(___ ay tyoon veel frahng saiz.)

a) Strasbourg (स्थ्राबूर्ग) (Strasbourg) (स्ट्रासबूर्ग) (Stras boor-guh)

b) Barcelone (बार्सलोन) (Barcelona) (बार्सलोना) (barce lone)

c) Hanoi (आनुआ) (Hanoi) (हानोए) (aa-nwah)

d) Madrid (माद्रीद) (Madrid) (मद्रिढ) (maa-drid)

Ans. (a) Strasbourg is the second city in France in terms of international congress and symposia, after Paris. It plays a major role as a business, commercial, and cultural centre in France.

2. द पोपस पैलेस___में स्थित है।

(The Pope's palace is situated in____)

(Le palais des papes se trouve à _____)

(ल पाले दे पाप स थ्रूव आ ___)

(Le palai de paap se truv aa ___)

a) Marseille (मारसेयी) (Marseille) (मारसेयी) (Maar-say-ee)

b) Paris (पारी) (Paris) (पैरिस) (Paari)

c) Avignon (आविन्यों) (Avignon) (आविन्यों) (Aa-vee-neo)

d) Lyon (लियों) (Lyon) (लियों) (Lee-ong)

Ans. (c) Palais Des Papes is the largest medieval gothic palace in the world. It came to symbolize the mighty influence of the Catholic Church.

3. यह महिला दूसरी से _____ है।

(This woman is ____ than the other.)

(Cette femme est ____ que l'autre.)

(सैत फाम ए ___ क लोथ्र।)

(seth faa-meu ay ___ kuh lo-tre.)

a) उतनी ही सुंदर (as handsome as) (aussi beau) (ओसी बो) (o si boh)

b) ज्यादा सुंदर (more beautiful) (plus belle) (प्लु बैल) (ploo bail)

c) कम सुंदर (less beautiful) (moins belles) (मुआं बैल) (moo-ang bail)

d) ज्यादा सुंदर (more handsome) (plus beau) (प्लु बो) (ploo boh)

Ans. (b) The French adverb plus has different pronunciations, depending on how it's used. Generally speaking, when plus has a positive meaning (e.g., more, extra, additional) it is pronounced [ploos]. When it is used as a negative adverb (meaning "no more"), it is usually pronounced [ploo].

4. मुझे कॉफी ___।

(I ___ some coffee.)

(Je ____ du café)

(ज ___ द्यु काफे।)

(Je ___ due kaa-fay.)

a) चाहता था (wanted) (voulu) (वुल्यु) (voo-lue)

b) चाहना (to want) (vouloir) (वुलुआर) (voo-loo-aar)

c) चाहुंगा (will want) (voudra) (वुध्रा) (voo-drah)

d) चाहिये (would like to have) (voudrais) (वुध्रे) (voo-dray)

Ans. (d) The meaning of "je voudrais" (pronounced: ʒə vudʀɛ) is "**I would like**". For example: "Je voudrais un croissant" (I'd like a croissant) or "Je voudrais acheter" (I'd like to buy). J'aimerais also means I'd like in French. This lesson covers how to say "I'd like" in French.

5. स्कूल वापस खुलना___
(Coming back is ___)
(La rentrée est _____
(ला रौंथ्रे ए ___)
(laa rahn-tray ay ___)

a) स्कूल का पहला दिन होता है। (first day of school) (le premier jour d'école) (ल प्रमिये जूर देकोल) (le pre-mee-ay joor day-kole)

b) स्कूल का आखिरी दिन होता है। (last day of school) (le dernier jour d'école) (ल दैर्नीये जूर देकोल) (le dair-nee-ay joor day-kole)

c) एक तरह का स्कूल का दिन होता है। (a type of school day) (une sorte de jour d'école) (युन सौर्त द जूर देकोल) (yoon-sor-tuh de joor day-kole)

d) एक फ्रैंच ट्रेन है। (a French train) (un train français) (अं थ्रां फ्रौंसे।) (ung trahng frahng-say)

Ans. (a) Premier (first) is treated like and adjective and must agree with the noun it modifies:

1. le premier jour d'école The first day of school.
2. ma première voiture My first car.
3. les premiers Américains The first Americans.
4. les premières nations The first nations.

6. वह जो सोसेज बेचता हो

(A person who sells sausages)

(une personne qui vend des saucisses)

(युन पैरसोन की वौं दे सोसीस)

(yoon paer-son kee vahng day so-see-seh)

a) कसाई (pork butcher) (charcuterie) (शारक्युतीए) (shaar-ku-tee-ay)

b) दर्जी (tailor) (tailleur) (ताइयर) (taa-ee-eur)

c) सामान बेचने वाला (seller) (vendeur) (वौंदर) (vahng-deuhr)

d) बेकर (baker) (boulanger) (बुलौंजे) (boo-lahng-jay)

Ans. (a) The word charcuterie originated in France, and it translates to "pork-butcher shop." While the original French translation refers to pork

7. कपड़े धोने के लिये, ___जाते हैं।

(To wash the clothes, we go to ___)

(Pour faire laver les vêtements, on va à _____)

(पूर फैर लावे ले वैतमौं, ओं वा आ ___)

(poor fayruh laa-vay lay vai-teh-mahng, ong vaa aa ___)

a) लौंड्री (the laundry) (la blanchisserie) (ला ब्लौंशिसरी) (laa blahng-shee-suh-ree)

b) फूल वाले के पास (to florist) (au fleuriste) (ओ फ्लरीस्त) (oh fluh-ree-stuh)

c) बाजार (to supermarket) (au supermarché) (ओ सुपैरमार्शे) (oh soo-pair-maar-shay)

d) मछली बाजार (to the fish market) (à la poissonnerie) (आ ला पुआसोनरी) (aa laa pwah-song-ree)

Ans. (a) blanchisserie

1. blanchisserie, la ~ (f) (lessivelinge) laundry, the ~ Noun.
2. blanchisserie, la ~ (f) cleaning industry,

8. जब मेरी बहन ने परीक्षा पास करी, उसने काम ___।

(When my sister passed her high school diploma, she ___a job.)

(Quand ma sœur a réussi le bac, elle _____ un emploi.) (कौं मा सर आ रेयुसी ल बाक, ऐल ___ अं नौंप्लुआ।)

(kahng maa ser aa ray-oo-see au baak, ail __ shair-shay ung ahng-plwah)

a) ढूँढेगी (will look) (chercherai) (शैशरि) (shair-shuh-ray)

b) ढूँढा (looked) (a cherché) (आ शैर्शे) (aa shair-shay)

c) ढूँढे रही है (looking) (cherche) (शैर्श) (shair-shuh)

d) ढूँढना (search) (chercher) (शैर्शे) (shair-shay)

Ans. (b) The French Baccalaureate or "le Bac", is an extensive, national examination taken at the end of the "Lycée" (High School), upon completion of 11th and 12th grade.

9. फ्रांस में सबसे अधिक आबादी वाला क्षेत्र ______ है।

(The most populated region in France is ___ .)

(La région la plus peuplée de France est ____.)

(ला रेजियों ला प्लु पप्ले द फ्रौंस ए___।)

(laa ray-jeong laa ploo peuh-play duh frahng-suh ay ___.)

a) मीदी पीरेने (Midi-Pyrénées) (Midi-Pyrénées) (मीदी पीरेने) (mee-dee pee-ray-nay)

b) ईल द फ्रौंस (Île-de-France) (Île-de-France) (ईल द फ्रौंस) (eel duh frahng-suh)

c) ब्रिटनी (Brittany) (Bretagne) (ब्रताऩ्य) (bruh-taa-nuh)

d) ओत सावुआ (Haute-Savoie) (Haute-Savoie) (ओत सावुआ) (oht saa-vwah)

Ans. (b) (Île-de-France is renowned for the large number of corporate headquarters located both in Paris and in the business district known as La Défense, just west of Neuilly. The région is a major tourist destination for international visitors.)

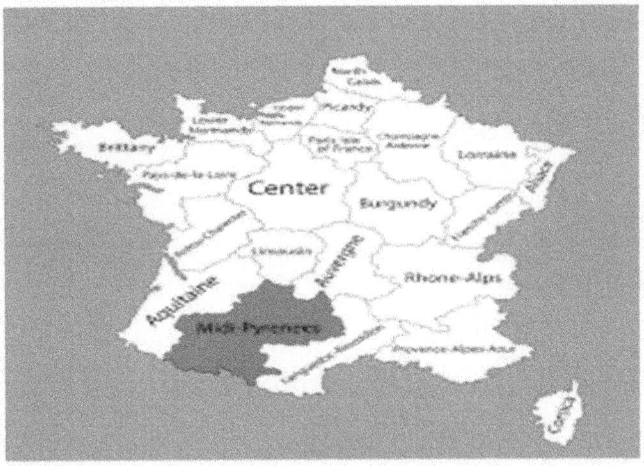

10. ____ 'हमेशा' का विपरीत है।

(____is the opposite of 'always'.)

(____ est le contraire de 'toujours'.)

(___ ए ल कोंथ्रैर द 'तूजूर'।)

(___ ay luh kong-trair duh too-joor.)

a) all the time (tout le temps) (तू ल तौं) (too luh tahng)

b) none (aucune) (ओक्युन) (oh-kyoon)

c) never (jamais) (जामे) (jaa-may)

d) without (sans) (सौं) (sahgn)

Ans. (c) Jamais = Never. The negative adverb ne … jamais means "never" or "not ever": Par exemple… Je n'ai ...

11. ____ जूतों की ____ कीमत क्या है?

(What is ____ price of ____ shoes?)

(Quel est ____ prix _____chaussures?)

(कैल ए ___ प्री ___ शोस्युर?)

(kail ay ___ pree ___ sho-sure ?)

a) द, द (the, the) (le, les) (ल, ले) (luh, lay)

b) ओफ द, ओफ द (of the, of the) (du, des) (द्यु, दे) (dyoo, day)

c) द, ओफ द (the, of the) (le, des) (ल, दे) (luh, day)

d) ओफ द, ओफ द (of the, of the) (du, des) (द्यु, दे) (dyoo, day)

Ans. (c) Unlike English, all nouns (words for things) in French are masculine or feminine.

1. Use le with masculine nouns.
2. Use la with feminine nouns.
3. Use l' with words of either gender that begin with a vowel or the letter h.

To describe an unspecified plural quantity, use "des" (both feminine and masculine), which tells you there is more than one item, but it is a vague plural quantity (it could be 2, could be 10,000 or more). This "des" usually applies to whole items, that you could count, but decided not to.

12. ___ एक फुटबॉल मैच आयोजित किया जाएगा।

(A football match will be held___.)

(Un match de foot aura lieu ___.)

(अं माच द फुत ओरा लिय ___।)

(ung maa-tch duh foot orah lee-uh ___.)

a) रेस्टोरेंट में (in the restaurant) (au restaurant) (ओ रेस्तरौं) (o ray-stuh-rahng)

b) थियेटर में (in the theatre) (au théâtre) (ओ तेआत्र) (o tay-aa-truh)

c) म्युजियम में (in the museum) (au musée) (ओ म्युज़े) (o myoo-zay)

d) मैदान में (in the stadium) (au stade) (ओ स्ताद) (o staa-duh)

Ans. (d) France's national football team represents the country in the international men's football tournaments. The French team is the reigning world champions.

13. आपने ____ स्कर्ट पहनी है?

(_____skirt are you wearing?)

(_____jupe portez-vous ?)

(___ ज्युप पोर्ते वू?)

(___jyoop por-tay voo?)

a) सी (which) (Quel) (केल) (kail)

b) कौनसी (which) (Quelle) (केल) (kail)

c) कौनसी (which) (Quel) (केल) (kail)

d) कौनसी (which) (Quelles) (केल) (kail)

Ans. (b) Quelle (or quelles in the plural) is an interrogative adjective (which? which ones?) or exclamation. It agrees in gender and number with the noun it.

14. देखो ____लोग भाग रहे हैं।

(Watch the people ____ are running.)

(Regardez les gens ____ courent.)

(रगार्दे ले जौं ___की कूर।)

(ruh-gaar-day lay jahng ____ koor.)

a) जो (who) (qui) (की) (kee)

b) वो (that) (qu') (क्) (kuh)

c) जब (when) (quand) (कौं) (kahng)

d) जहाँ (where) (où) (उ) (oo)

Ans. (a) Qui is a subject pronoun, it replaces the subject of the sentence. Example: Je prends le train. Le train va à Paris. I'm taking the train.

15. मुझे संदेह है कि वह परीक्षा में ___ ।)

(I doubt that he ___ the exam.)

(Je doute qu'il ____ l'examen)

(ज दूत किल____ लेगज़ामां।)

(juh doot keel ___ lay gza-mang.)

a) सफल हुआ (pass) (réussit) (रेयुसी) (ray-yoo-see)

b) सफल होगा (will pass) (réussisse) (रेयुसीस) (ray-yoo-sees)

c) सफल होगा (will pass) (réussisses) (रेयुसीस) (ray-yoo-sses)

d) सफल हो चुका (pass) (a réussi) (आ रेयुसी) (ray-yoo-see)

Ans. (b) Learn how to conjugate réussir, a regular–ir French verb. This includes conjugations of the subjunctive, imperfect, and imperative tenses.

16. rqe d{kk ls _______ D;¨a vk,

(Why did you _________ of the class?)

(Pourquoi tu ________ de la class?)

¼iqjdqvk R;q _____ n yk Dykl\½

(Poor-kwa tu ________ duh laa klaas?)

a) ckgj (come out) (es sorti) ¼, l¨rÊ ½ (ay sortee)

b) ckgj (come out) (es sortis) ¼, l¨rÊ½ (ay sortee)

c) ckgj (come out) (est sorti) ¼, l¨rÊ½ (ay sortee)

d) ckgj (come out) (as sorti) ¼, l¨rÊ½ (ay sortee)

Ans. (a) In the sentence "Je suis sorti," for instance, you can see that I am what went out, and I am also what's out at the end of the sentence. The use of the auxiliary être also means that the subject will agree with the past participle.

17. ge _______ laxhr ctk jgs gSaA

(We are making _________ music.)

(On fait ________ musique.)

¼v¨a Q¢ _____ E;qt+hdA½

(ong fay _____ muzeek.)

a) dqN (some) (du) ¼n~;q½ (dyoo)

b) dqN (some) (de la) ¼n yk½ (duh-laa)

c) dqN (some) (de) ¼n½ (duh)

d) dqN (some) (d') ¼n½ (duh)

Ans. (b) Du, de la, de l', des = Unspecified Quantity — de la (+ feminine word),; de l' (followed by a vowel),; des (+ plural word).

18. dy vkleku LysVh _______ A

(Yesterday, the sky _______ grey.)

(Hier, le ciel ________ gris.)

¼b;Sj] y fl;Sy _____ ÄzhA½

(ee-air, luh see-ail ________ ghree.)

a) Fkk (was) (était) ¼,srs½ (ay-tay)

b) Fkk (had) (avait) ¼vkos½ (aa-vay)

c) Fkk (was) (étais) ¼,srs½ (ay-tay)

d) Fkk (had) (avaient) ¼vkos½ (aa-vay)

Ans. (a) Translations in context of "était" in French-English from Reverso Context: était très, était nécessaire, était déjà, était trop, était également.

19. foDVj º;qx¨ dh e`R;q dgk¡ gqÃ Fkh

(Where did Victor Hugo die?)

(Où est mort Victor Higo?)

¼Å , e©j foDrj ;qx¨\½

(oo ay mor veek-tor yugo?)

a) cst+©al¨a (Besançon) (Besançon) ¼cst+©al¨a½ (Bay-Zang-Song)

b) iSfjl (Paris) (Paris) ¼ikjh½ (Paa-ree)

c) :v¨a (Rouen) (Rouen) ¼:v¨a½ (Roo-ahng)

d) fy;¨a (Lyon) (Lyon) ¼fy;¨a½ (Lee-yong)

Ans. (a) Besançon is the historical capital of watchmaking in France. This has led it to become a centre for innovative companies in the fields of microtechno-logy.

20. eSaus _______ isVª¨y [kjhnk _______ xkM+h d¢ fy,A

(I bought _______ petrol for _______ car.)

(J'ai acheté _____ essence pour _______ voiture.)

¼ts vk"krs ______ ,sl©al iwj ______ oqvkP;qjA½

(Jay aa-sh-tay ______ ay-sahngs poor _______ vwa-chur.)

a) dqN] esjh (some, my) (de l', ma) ¼n~ y~] ek½ (duh-luh, maa)

b) dqN] esjh (of, my) (de, mon) ¼n~] e¨a½ (duh, mang)

c) dqN] esjh (some, my) (du, ma) ¼n~;q] ek½ (dyoo, maa)

d) dqN] esjh (my, some) (ma, de l') ¼ek] n~ y~½ (maa, duh-luh)

Ans. (a) If the thing/person is masculine (le), then you generally use mon to translate 'my'; if the thing/ person is feminine (la), then you generally use ma to translate 'my'; if the thing/person is plural (les), then you use mes to translate 'my'.

21. mlus n¨ vaMs _______ v©j mlus mUgsa _____ A

(She _______ two eggs and he ________ them.)

(Elle _______ deux oeufs et il les ________.)

¼,sy _____ n t+ , by yst ______ A½

(ail _______ duh zuh ay eel layz __________.)

a) fy,] r¨M+ fn;k (took, broke) (a pris, a cassés) ¼vk izh] vk dkls½ (aa pree, aa kasay)

b) r¨M+ fn;k] fy, (broke, took) (a cassés, a pris) ¼vk dkls] vk izh½ (aa-kasay, aa pree)

c) fy,] r¨M+ fn;k (took, broke) (a pris, as cassés) ¼vk izh] vk dkls½ (aa pree, aa kasay)

d) fy,] r¨M+ fn;k (took, broke) (as pris, a cassés) ¼vk izh] vk dkls½ (aa pree, aa kasay)

Ans. (a) The French verb casser literally means "to break" and is also used in many idiomatic expressions. The verb is used to talk about breaking.

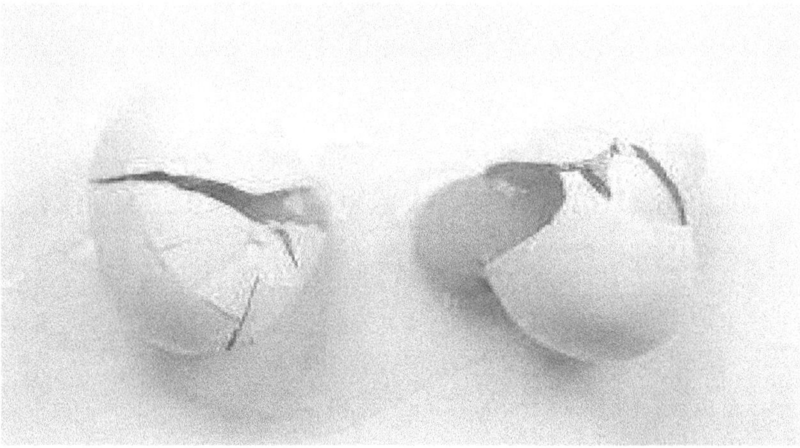

22. jus x¨lhuh _______ gSA

(René Goscinny is ________.)

(René Goscinny est ________.)

¼jus x¨lhuh , _____ A½

(Ruh-nay Go-see-nee ay ________.)

a) ,syftfj;u (Algerian) (algérien) ¼vkytsfj;k¡½ (aal-jay-ree-ang)

b) cSyft;u (Belgian) (belge) ¼cSYt½ (Bail-ge)

c) lqbl (Swiss) (suisse) ¼lqbl½ (Soo-iss)

d) ÝSap (French) (français) ¼Ý©als½ (frahgn-Say)

Ans. (d) René Goscinny was a French comic editor and writer. He created the Astérix comic book seris with illustrator Albert Uderzo.

23. fo'ke dh igpku djsaA

(Spot the odd one.)

(Chassez l'intrus.)

¼"kkls ySaFkzqlA½

(shaa-say lain-troos)

a) dSEecVZ (Camembert) (Camembert) ¼dke©acSj½ (Kaa-mahng-bair)

b) j¨dQ¨VZ (Roquefort) (Roquefort) ¼j¨dQ¨j½ (Roke-for)

c) cjxaMh (Burgundy) (Bourgogne) ¼cqjx¨U;½ (Boor-go-nyu)

d) czh (Brie) (Brie) ¼Òzh½ (Bree)

Ans. (c) Bourgogne is a region in France whose wines are famous all around the world.

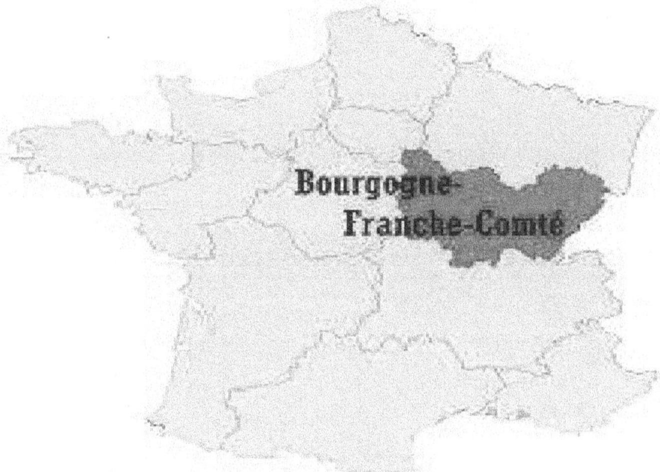

24. Ýkal ,d _____ gSA

(France is a _____.)

(La France est une _______.)

¼yk Ý©al , R;qu _____ A½

(Laa frahgn-se ay tune ______.)

a) x.kra= (Republic) (République) ¼jsl;qfCyd½ (Ray-publeek)

b) lkezkT; (Monarchy) (Monarchie) ¼e¨uk"kÊ½ (Mo-naar-she)

c) "kgj (city) (ville) ¼ohy½ (veel)

d) }hi (island) (île) ¼Ãy½ (eel)

Ans. (a) republic [noun] (a country with) a form of govern-ment in which there is no king or queen, the power of govern-ment, law-making etc.

Liberté • Égalité • Fraternité

RÉPUBLIQUE FRANÇAISE

25. lqanj dk foy¨e _______ g¨rk gSA

(The opposite of 'handsome' is ______.)

(Le contraire de 'beau' est _______.)

¼y d©aFkzSj n 'c¨' , ______ A½

(Luh kang-traire duh bo ay _______.)

a) lqanj (handsome) (Beau) ¼c¨½ (Bo)

b) dq:i (ugly) (laid) ¼ys½ (Lay)

c) lqanj (beautiful) (belle) ¼cSy½ (Bail)

d) N¨Vk (small) (petit) ¼ifr½ (puh-tee)

Ans. (b) Laid. adjective. homely [adjective] (American) (of a person) not attractive; ugly. ugly [adjective] unplea-sant to look at.

26. vkfyt+s d¨jus _______ [ksyrh gSA

(Alizé Cornet pratices ________.)

(Alizé Cornet pratique le/ la _______.)

¼आलिज़े कोर्ने प्रातीक ल/ला_____ A½

(aa-lee-zay kor-nay pra-teek luh/laa _____.)

a) Vsful (tennis) (tennis) ¼rsuhl½ (tay-nees)

b) fØd¢V (cricket) (cricket) ¼Øhd¢r½ (Kree-kait)

c) QqVckWy (football) (foot) ¼Qwr½ (foot)

d) ckWfDlax (boxing) (boxe) ¼c¨Dl½ (Box)

Ans. (a) Alizé Cornet is a French professional tennis player.

27. ÑI;k] Dykl ls _______ fudysaA

(_______ of the class, please.)

(_______ de la classe, s'il vous plaît.)

¼_____ n yk Dykl] fly ow lysA½

(________ duh laa klass, sil-voo-plai.)

a) ckgj (get out) (sors) ¼l©j½ (sor)

b) ckgj (lets get out) (sortons) ¼l©jr¨a½ (sor-tang)

c) ckgj (go out) (sortez) ¼l©jrs½ (sor-tay)

d) vki ckgj (you go out) (vous sortez) ¼ow l©jrs½ (voo-sortay)

Ans. (c) Using Sortir in French — sortir de means "to get out of" or "to leave": As in, Tu dois sortir de l'eau (You need to get out of the water).

28. vxj rqe tYnh _______] r¨ ge flusek pysaxsA

(If you _______ early, we will go to movies.)

(Si tu ______ tôt, on ira au cinema.)

¼lh R;q _____ r¨] v¨a uhjk v¨ flusekA½

(See tyoo ______ toh, ang neera o see-nay-maa)

a) pkgrs (want) (veus) ¼o½ (vuh)

b) vk, Fks (have come) (est venue) ¼, oU;q½ (ay vuh-nue)

c) vk, (come) (vient) ¼fo;ka½ (vee-yang)

d) vk, (come) (viens) ¼fo;ka½ (vee-yang)

Ans. (d) Venir is commonly used to express the recent past — the idea that one has just done something. This construction is formed with the conjugated venir + de + the infinitive of the action that has just occurred. Je viens d'arriver / I (have) just arrived. Ils viennent de déjeuner / They just ate lunch.

29. o¨ _______ xyh ugÈ tkurkA

(He doesn’t know ______ street.)

(Il ne connaît pas ______ rue.)

¼by u d¨us ik ______ j;qA½

(eel nuh konay paa ______ rooh.)

a) ;g (this) (ce) ¼l½ (suh)

b) ;g (this) (cet) ¼lSr½ (sait)

c) ;g (this) (cette) ¼lSr½ (sait)

d) ;g (this) (ces) ¼ls½ (say)

Ans. (c) You use cette before a singular, feminine noun. The noun can begin with a vowel or a consonant, it doesn't matter. You would still use cette. Ex: Cette fille est belle.

30. iSfjl fdl {ks= esa fLFkr gS

(Paris is situated in which region?)

(Paris se trouve dans quelle région?)

¼ikjh l Fkzqo n©a dSy jsft;¨a\½

(Paa-ree suh troov dahng kail ray-geong?)

a) Ýkal dk }hi (island of France) (île de France) ¼Ãy n Ý©al½ (eel duh france)

b) e¨jhf“k;l }hi (Mauritius island) (île Maurice) ¼Ãy e¨fjl½ (eel mo-rees)

c) ¨lÊdk }hi (Corsica island) (île de Corse) ¼Ãy n d¨lZ½ (eel duh kors)

d) xqvknywi (Guadeloupe) (La Guadeloupe) ¼yk xqvknywi½ (Laa Gwad-loop)

Ans. (a) Île-de-France is bounded by the régions of Hauts-de-France to the north, Grand Est to the east, Bourgogne-Franche-Comté to the southeast, Centre to the south.

31. eSaus Vhoh _______ [kkuk [kk;kA

(I ate dinner _______ T.V.)

(J'ai diné _______ la télé.)

¼ts nhus _____ yk rsysA½

(Jay dee-nay _____ laa tay-lay)

a) ns[k jgk gwi (watch) (regarde) ¼jxkZn½ (ruh-gaard)

b) ns[krs gq, (while watching) (en regardant) ¼v©a jxknZv¨a½ (ahng ruh-gaardahng)

d) ns[kuk (to watch) (regarder) ¼jxknsZ½ (ruh-gaar-day)

e) ns[kk Fkk (have watched) (ai regardé) ¼, jxknsZ½ (ay-ruh-gaarday)

Ans. (b) The verb 'regarder,' means 'to watch' and 'to look at' in English.

32. _______ ,d [ksy gSA

(_______ is a sport.)

(______ est un sport.)

¼______,s rka Li©jA½

(ay-tang spor.)

a) Vsuhl (tennis) (Le tennis) ¼y rsuhl½ (Luh tay-nees)

b) dkj “ks;jÈx (car sharing) (La covoiturage) ¼y d¨oqvkP;qjkt½ (Luh ko-vwa-chu-raage)

c) cqycqys (the bubbles) (Les bulles) ¼ys C;qy½ (Lay byool)

d) ikjdj (Parkour) (Le Parkour) ¼y ikjdwj½ (Luh Paar-koor)

Ans. (a) How to say tennis in French; chaussure de tennis; play tennis; jouer au tennis.

33. xqLrko bQSy ,d _______ FkkA

(Gustave Eiffel was an _______.)

(Gustave Eiffel était ______.)

¼xqLrko bQSy ,rs ______ A½

(Gus-taav eefail ay-tay _______.)

a) ewfrZdkj (Sculptor) (Sculpteur) ¼lD;qyrj½ (Skyool-teur)

b) isaVj (Painter) (Peintre) ¼iSaFkz½ (Pahg-tre)

c) jl¨b;k (Chef) (Cuisinier) ¼D;qft+fu;s½ (Kyoo-zee-niay)

d) bathuh;j (engineer) (ingénieur) ¼,satsfu;j½ (ang-jay-near)

Ans. (a) The Eiffel tower was built by Gustave Eiffel and his team for 1889 World fair.

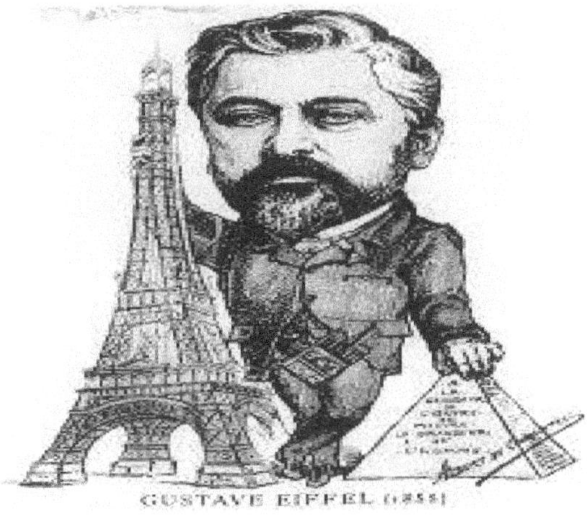

34. dkjyk Òzquh ,d izfl) _______ gSA

(Carla Bruni is a famous ________.)

(Carla Bruni est une ______ célèbre.)

¼dkjyk Òzquh , R;qu _____ lsySÒzA½

(Kaar-la Broo-ni ay tune _____ say-lai-bre.)

a) xk;d (Singer) (Chanteuse) ¼“k©art+½ (Shahng-tuh-zuh)

b) dfo (Poete) (Poète) ¼i¨;Sr½ (Po-ait)

c) vkfdZVsDV (Architect) (Architecte) ¼vkjf"krsDr½ (aar-she-tect)

d) ysf[kdk (Writer) (écrivaine) ¼,[kzhoSu½ (ay-khree-vaine)

Ans. (a) She is also the wife of former French President Nicolas Sarkozy.

35. ßys i©alsÞ fdrkc fdlus fy[kh gS

(Who wrote the book "The Pensées"?)

(Qui a écrit "Les Pensées"?)

¼dh vk ,[kzh ys i©als\½

(Kee aa ay-khree lay pahng-say?)

a) xqLrko ¶y¨cSrZ (Gustave Flaubert) (Gustave Flaubert) ¼xqLrko ¶y¨cSj½ (Goos-taav flow-bair)

b) foDVj º;qx¨ (Victor Hugo) (Victor Hugo) ¼foDrj b;qx¨½ (Victor you-go)

c) cyst+ ikldky (Blaise Pascal) (Blaise Pascal) ¼cyst+ ikLdky½ (Blaize Pass-kaal)

d) o¨yrSj (Voltaire) (Voltaire) ¼o¨yrSj½ (Vol-taire)

Ans. (a) Blaise Pascal (1623-1662), French Philosopher and Scientist, was one of the greatest mathematicians of all time.

36. _______ & ugÈ] vÒh rd ugÈA

(________ – No, not yet.)

(______ – Non, pas encore)

¼______ & u¨a] ik t+©ad¨jA½

(_______ – No, paa zahng-kor.)

a) rqe dgkį jgrs g¨\ (Where do you live?) (où habites-tu?) ¼Å vkchr R;q\½ (oo aabeet tyoo?)

b) D;k rqe y ywoz x, g¨\ (Have you visited The Louvre?) (As-tu visité le Louvre?) ¼vk R;q fot+hrs y ywoz\½ (aa tyoo vizitay luh loovre?)

c) e©le dSlk gS\ (How is the weather?) (Quel temps fait-il?) ¼dSy r©a Q¢&fry\½ (Kail-tahng fay-til?)

d) le; D;k gqvk gS\ (what time is it?) (Quelle heure est-il?) ¼dSy vj , fry\½ (kail err ay-til?)

Ans. (b) The Louvre or the Louvre Museum is the world's most-visited museum, and a historic landmark in Paris, France. It is the home of some of the best-known work.

37. ________ ,d ÝSap v[kckj gSA

(______ is a French newspaper.)

(______ est un journal français.)

(______, तां tqjuky Ý©alsA½

(______ ay tung joor-naal frahng-say.)

a) fo"o (The world) (Le monde) ¼y e¨an½ (Luh mong-duh)

b) i`Foh (The earth) (La terre) ¼yk rSj½ (Laa-tair)

c) "kgj (The city) (La ville) ¼yk ohy½ (Laa Veel)

d) {ks= (The region) (La région) ¼yk jsth;¨a½ (Laa ray-giong)

Ans. (a) Le Monde, (French: "The World") daily newspaper published in Paris, one of the most important and widely respected newspapers in the world.

38. esjs ________ckgj er tkukA

(Don't go out ______ me.)

(Ne sortez pas ______ moi.)

¼u l¨rsZ ik _____ eqvkA½

(Nuh sor-tay paa _____ mwa.)

a) ;gk¡ (at) (chez) ¼"ks½ (shay)

b) }kjk (by) (par) ¼ikj½ (paar)

c) tcls (since) (depuis) ¼niqb½ (Duh-pooi)

d) fcuk (without) (sans) ¼l©a½ (sahng)

Ans. (d) Use 'sans' expressions. The French preposition sans means "without," indicating a lack in general, an absence, privation or an exclusion. It can be used with nouns, pronouns, and verbs, and it appears in many French idiomatic expressions: to signify "without," to express a condition and to use with an infinitive.

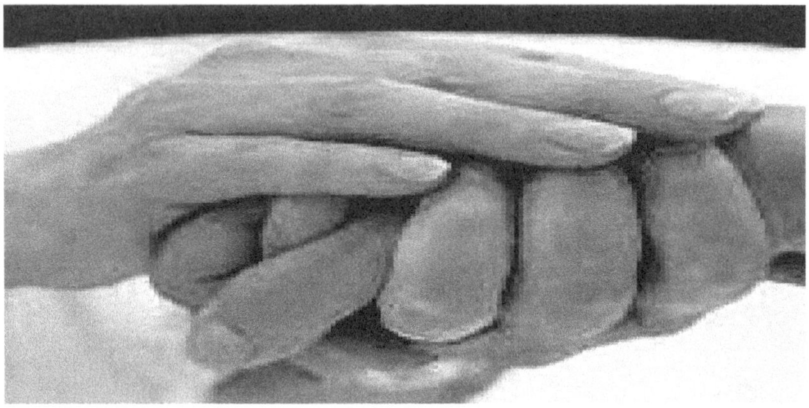

39. mld¢ nk¡r esa nnZ gS] og nk¡r¨a d¢ MkWDVj ________ tk jgk gSA

(He has pain in his teeth, he is going ______ dentist.)

(Il a mal aux dents, il va ________ le dentiste)

(by vk eky v¨ n©a] by ok _____ y n©afrLrA½

(eel aa maal o Dahng, eel vaa _____ luh dahng-tist.)

a) d¢ ;gk¡ (at) (chez) ¼"ks½ (shay)

b) vanj (inside) (dans) ¼n©a½ (dahng)

c) Åij (on) (sur) ¼L;qj½ (syoor)

d) ikl esa (at the side of) (à coté de) ¼vk d¨rs n½ (aa kotay duh)

Ans. (a) In French language, two prepositions can be used while talking about "going to a place": à (to, at) and chez (at). 'Chez' is generally used when talking about a person's place.

40. rqe ogk¡ vDlj tkrs g¨\& _________ A

(You go there often? – ______.)

(Tu y vas souvent? – _______)

(R;q b ok lqo¨a\ ______ A½

(Tyoo ee va soo-vahng? – __________.)

a) ugÈ] eSa ogk¡ dÒh ugÈ tkrkA (No, I never go there.) (Non, Je ny vais jamais.) ¼u¨a] t uh os tkesA½ (No, Juh nee vay jaa-may.)

b) ugÈ] eSa tkrk ugÈ ogk¡ dÒhA (No, I never there go.) (Non, Je ne vais y jamais.) ¼u¨a] t u os b tkesA½ (No, Juh nuh vay ee Jaa-may.)

c) ugÈ] eSa ogk¡ dqN ugÈ tkrkA (No, I nothing go there.) (Non, Je ny vais rien) ¼u¨a] t uh os jh;k¡A½ (No, juh nee vay ri-ang)

d) ugÈ] eSa tkrk gw¡A (No, I go.) (Non, ny vais.) ¼u¨a] th os½ (No, jee vay)

Ans. (a) Jamais = Never. The negative adverb ne … jamais means "never" or "not ever".

Chapter 2

1. rqEgkjs ________ [;ky fnypLi gSaA

(_______ your ideas are interesting.)

(_______ vos idées sont intéressantes.)

(______ o¨ vhns l¨a rSarsjSl¨arA½

(_______ vo zeeday song tai-ray-sont.)

a) lkjs (All) (Tout) ¼rw½ (Too)

b) lkjs (All) (Tous) ¼rw½ (Too)

c) lkjs (All) (Toute) ¼rwr½ (Toot)

d) lkjs (All) (Toutes) ¼rwr½ (Toot)

Ans. (d) There are different ways to use tout in French - as a pronoun, an adjective or an adverb - to express slightly different things:

1. Tout = everything.
2. Tout/tous/toute/toutes + [article] + [chose(s)]= All + [article] + [things]/[article] whole [thing(s)]
3. Tous / toutes = all [of them]
4. Tout + [adverbe] = Very + [adverb]

2. Þn LVªsatjß fdlus fy[kh gS

(Who wrote "The Stranger"?)

(Qui a écrit << L'Étranger >> ?)

¼dh vk ,[kzh Þys Fkz©tsasß\½

(kee aa ay-khree lay-trahng-jay ?)

a) vkycVZ dSE;ql (Albert Camus) (Albert Camus) ¼vkycSj dkE;q½ (aal-bair kaa-myoo)

b) lkrZ (Sartre) (Sartre) ¼lkFkz½ (Saartre)

c) i¨y ,yqvknZ (Paul Eluard) (Paul Éluard) ¼i¨y ,yqvkj½ (Paul ay-loo-aar)

d) oSjySu (Verlaine) (Verlaine) ¼oSjySu½ (Vair-laine)

Ans. (a) Albert Camus was a French philosopher, author, dramatist and journalist. He was awarded the 1957 Nobel Prize in Literature at the age of 44.

3. Òwrdky esa cnysa& eSa dkWQh ihuk pkgrh gw¡A

(Change into past tense– I want to drink coffee.)

(Mettez au passé– Je veux boire du café.)

¼esrs v¨ ikls & t o cqvkj n~;q dkQ¢A½

(Mai-tai o paa-say – Je vuh bwar dyoo kaafay.)

a) eq>s dkWQh ihuh FkhA (I wanted drink coffee.) (Je voulu bu du café.) ¼t oqY;q C;q dkQ¢A½ (Je voo-lyoo byoo dyoo kaa-fay.)

b) eSa dkWQh ihuk pkgrh FkhA (I wanted to drink coffee.) (J'ai voulu boire du café.) ¼ts oqY;q cqvkj n~;q dkQ¢A½ (Jay voo-lyoo bwar dyoo kaa-fay.)

c) eSa dkWQh ihuk pkgrh gw¡A (I am wanted to drink coffee.) (Je suis voulu boire café.) ¼t lwb oqY;q cqvkj dkQ¢A½ (Je sooi voo-lyoo bwar kaa-fay.)

d) eSaus dkWQh ihrs gq, ns[khA (I saw drinking coffee.) (J'ai vu boire du café.) ¼ts O;q cqvkj n~;q dkQ¢A½ (Jay vyoo bwar dyoo kaa-fay.)

Ans. (b) In French, the past tense works basically the same way as in English. It is also formed by two words just like its English counterpart by using the verb avoir (in most cases) which means 'to have', or être which means 'to be' before the main verb.

4. _______ g¨us okyh gSA viuk Nkrk ys y¨A

(It's going ______. Take your umbrella.)

(Il va _____. Prends ton parapluie.)

¼by ok _____ A iz©a r¨a ikjklyqÃA½

(eel vaa ______. Prahng tang para-ploo-ee.)

a) ckrsa djuk (to talk) (bavarder) ¼ckokjns½ (Baa-vaar-day)

b) ckjh"k g¨uk (to rain) (Pleuvoir) ¼lyoqvkj½ (Pluh-voo-aar)

c) dkfcy g¨uk (to be able to) (Pouvoir) ¼iqoqvkj½ (Poo-voo-aar)

d) tkuk (to leave) (partir) ¼ikjrhj½ (Paar-teer)

Ans. (b) Meaning "to rain," the French verb "pleuvoir" is an easy one to study.

5. ge chp ij ________ ys jgs gSaA

(We are ______ on the beach.)

(Nous ______ à la plage.)

¼uw _____ vk yk lyktA½

(Noo ______ aa laa plaage.)

a) vkuan (enjoying) (nous amusons) ¼uw t+kE;qt+©½ (Noo zamyoo-zahng)

b) vkuan (enjoying) (amusais) ¼vkE;qt+s½ (aa-myoo-zay)

c) vkuan (enjoying) (amusons) ¼vkE;qt+¨a½ (aa-myoo-zahng)

d) vkuan (enjoying) (samusons) ¼lkE;qt+¨a½ (saa-myoo-zahng)

Ans. (a) amuser ; amuse [verb] to make (someone) laugh. The children were amused by the monkey's antics. ; amuse [verb] to interest or give pleasure to.

6. og cl ________ Ldwy tkrk gSA

(He goes to school _____ bus.)

(Il va à l'école _____ bus.)

¼by ok vk ysd¨y _____ C;qlA½

(eel vaa aa lay-kole ______ byoos.)

a) esa (in) (en) ¼v©a½ (ahng)

b) }kjk (by) (par) ¼ikj½ (paar)

c) rd (to the) (à la) ¼vk yk½ (aa-laa)

d) Åij (on) (sur) ¼L;qj½ (syoor)

Ans. (a) We use "en" in French to replace a noun modified by a notion of quantity. En in French is usually translated into of it or about it. But be careful, in English you can sometimes drop the "of it", but in French you should never drop.

7. vxj og vius ikB________]r¨ og xyfr;k¡ ugÈ djrkA

(If he ____ his lessons, he would not do the mistakes.)

(Sil ______ ses leçons, il ne ferait pas de fautes.)

¼fly _____ ls yl¨a] by u Qjs ik n Q¨uA½

(sil ______ say duh-sang, eel nuh feray paa duh fot.)

a) i<+s (read) (apprenais) ¼vkizus½ (aa-pruh-nay)

b) i<+uk (to study) (apprendre) ¼vkiz©an½ (aa-prahng-dre)

c) i<+rk gksrk (read) (apprenait) ¼vkizus½ (aa-pruh-nay)

d) i<+uk (read) (apprend) ¼vkiz©a½ (aa-prahng)

Ans. (c) To express "to learn how to [do]" in French, you will use "apprendre à + [infinitif]"

8. ________ Ýk¡l esa iSnk ugÈ gqvkA

(______ was not born in France.)

(______n'est pas né en France.)

¼ _____ us ik us v©a Ý©alA½

(______ nay paa nay ahng France.)

a) foDVj g~;wx¨ (Victor Hugo) (Victor Hugo) ¼foDrj ;qx¨½ (Victor Ugo)

b) vkysDt+¨anz M;qekl (Alexandre Dumas) (Alexandre Dumas) ¼vkysXt+©aèkz n~;qek½ (Alek-Zahng-dre Dyoo-maa)

c) T;qYl oSuZ (Jules Verne) (Jules Verne) ¼T;qy oSuZ½ (Jyool Vairne)

d) j¨cVZ ,saMjlu (Robert Anderson) (Robert Anderson) ¼j¨cSj v©anSjlSu½ (Robair ahng-dair-son)

Ans. (d) Robert Anderson was a 19th century Scottish inventor, best known for inventing the first crude electric carriage in Scotland.

9. 'Å¡pk' dk foy¨e "kCn D;k gS

(What is the opposite of 'High'?)

(Quel est le contraire de 'Haute'?)

¼dSy , y d¨aFkzSj n 'v¨r'\½

(kail ay luh kong-traire duh oht?)

a) Luku (Bath) (Bain) ¼ckj½ (Bang)

b) uhpk (Low) (Bas) ¼ck½ (Baa)

c) vPNk (Good) (Bien) ¼fc;kj½ (Bee-ang)

d) csap (Bench) (Banc) ¼c©ad½ (Bonk)

Ans. (b) French à bas (literally "to the bottom").

10. vkt l¨Qh ,d fQYe ________ A

(Today, Sophie ______ a movie.)

(Aujourd'hui, Sophie _______ un film.)

¼v¨t©jnqÃ] l¨Qh _____ vj fQYeA½

(O-Jor-dui, Sophie ______ ang film.)

a) ns[kus tk,xhA (is going to watch) (va voir) ¼ok वुआर½ (vaa-voo-aar)

b) ns[kus tk,xh (is going to watch) (vas voir) ¼ok वुआर½ (vaa-voo-aar)

c) ns[kuk (to see) (voir) ¼ वुआर½ (voo-aar)

d) tkrh gS (going) (va) ¼ok½ (vaa)

Ans. (a) In a general sense, voir means "to see" as in, "Je vois Lise le samedi." (I see Lise on Saturdays.) or "Je vois deux chiens." (I see two dogs.).

11. rqe ________ cts mBrs g¨

(You wake up ______ what time?)

(Tu te réveilles ______ quelle heure?)

¼R;q r jsoÃ _____ dSy vj\½

(Tyoo tuh Ray-vee______ kail err?)

a) vanj (in) (en) ¼v©a½ (ahng)

b) fdrus (at) (à) ¼vk½ (aa)

c) }kjk (from) (de) ¼n½ (duh)

d) Åij (on) (sur) ¼L;qj½ (syoor)

Ans. (b) The most common usage of the preposition à is to mean "to" or "at" when following the verb aller (to go). When ais followed by le, la, les (the), a contraction must occur. For example, "Je vais au (à + le) magasin" (I go to the store). This page covering the French articles covers these contractions in detail.

12. ;g thj¨e ________ xkM+h gSA

(This is the car ______ Jérome.)

(C'est la voiture _____ Jérome.)

¼ls yk oqvkP;qj _____ tsj¨eA½

(Say laa vwa-ture ____ Jay-rome.)

a) dh (at) (à) ¼vk½ (aa)

b) vanj (in) (en) ¼v©a½ (ahng)

c) dh (of) (de) ¼n½ (duh)

d) lkFk (with) (avec) ¼आवेक½ (aa-vaik)

Ans. (c) The French preposition de is required after certain verbs and phrases when they are followed by an infinitive. And de is required after many French verbs and phrases that need an indirect object, Keep in mind that de plus a noun can be replaced by the adverbial pronoun en. For example, J'en ai besoin. > I need it.

13. rqe LVs"ku ______ tkrs g¨

(_____ do you go to the station?)

(_______ vas-tu à la gare?)

¼ _____ ok&R;q vk yk xkj\½

(Komo vaa tyoo aa laa gaar?)

a) dSls (How) (comment) ¼d¨e¨a½ (komo)

b) d©uls (Which) (quel) ¼dSy½ (kail)

c) d©u (Who) (qui) ¼dh½ (kee)

d) fdrus (How many) (combien) ¼d¨afc;kj½ (ko bee-yang)

Ans. (a) Comment is the French equivalent of "how." Here are some examples:

1. Comment vas-tu? > How are you? (Literally, "how are you going?")
2. Comment as-tu fait ça? How did you do that?

14. ogki ________ gS

(_______ is there?)

(______ est là?)

¼ ______ , yk\½

(_____ ay laa?)

a) dgki (where) (où) ¼Å½ (oo)

b) d©u (who) (qui) ¼dh½ (kee)

c) dSls (how) (comment) ¼d¨e¨½ (komo)

d) d©ulh (which) (quel) ¼dSy½ (kail)

Ans. (b) Qui is a subject pronoun, it replaces the subject of the sentence. Example: Je prends le train. Le train va à Paris. I'm taking the train.

Who's there

15. eq>s ________ isafly pkfg,A

(I want ______ pencils.)

(Je veux _______ crayons.)

¼t o ______ [kzs;¨aA½

(Juh vuh _______ krai-yong.)

a) dqN (some) (des) ¼ns½ (day)

b) dqN (some) (du) ¼n~;q½ (dyoo)

c) dqN (some) (de l') ¼n~ y~½ (duh-luh)

d) dqN (some) (de la) ¼n yk½ (duh-laa)

Ans. (a) To describe an unspecified plural quantity, use "des" (both feminine and masculine), which tells you there is more than one item, but it is a vague plural quantity (it could be 2, could be 10,000 or more). This "des" usually applies to whole items, that you could count, but decided not to.

16. ;g cPp¨a ________ dejk gSA

(This is the room ______ children.)

(C'est la chambre ______ enfants.)

¼ls yk "k©aÒz _____ v©aQ¨aA½

(Say laa shahng-bre _______ ahng-fahng.)

a) dk (of the) (des) ¼ns½ (day)

b) dk (of the) (du) ¼n~;q½ (dyoo)

c) dk (of the) (de l') ¼n~ y~½ (duh-luh)

d) dk (of the) (de la) ¼n~ yk½ (duh-laa)

Ans. (a) Here 'des' is not a definite article. It is an "article contracté" (contracted article) i.e. de + les = des (of the).

17. ge ________ vH;kl dk;Z dj jgs gSaA

(We are doing ______ exercises.)

(Nous faisons ______ exercices.)

¼uw Qt+¨a ______ ,xtSjflt+A½

(Noo fuh-zang ______ egg-zair-seez.)

a) gekjk (our) (notre) ¼u¨Fkz½ (no-tre)

b) gekjs (our) (nos) ¼u¨½ (no)

c) rqEgkjs (your) (vos) ¼o¨½ (vo)

d) rqEgkjk (your) (votre) ¼o¨Fkz½ (vo-tre)

Ans. (b) Note that notre maison is singular because there is only one house that we share, while nos voitures is plural because we each have a car.

18. rqe ________ dqÙks d¨ Äqekrs g¨A

(You are walking ______ dog.)

(Tu promène ______ chienne.)

¼R;q iz¨eSu _____ f"k;SuA½

(Tyoo pro-maine ______ she-yaine.)

a) mldh (her) (sa) ¼lk½ (saa)

b) viuh (your) (ta) ¼rk½ (taa)

c) viuk (your) (ton) ¼r¨a½ (tong)

d) mldk (his) (son) ¼l¨a½ (song)

Ans. (c) Chienne is a female dog.

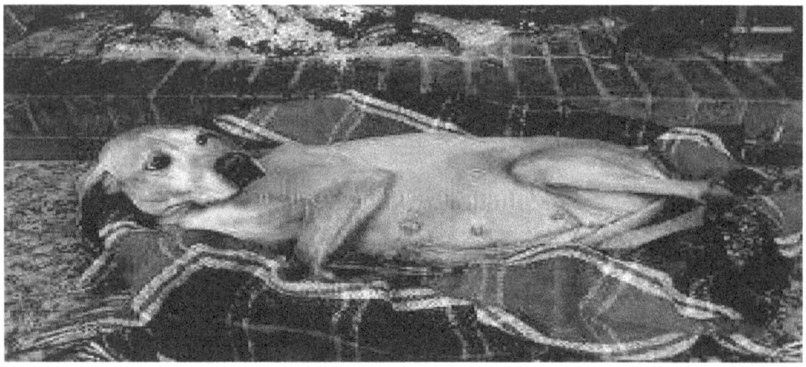

19. fo'ke dh igpku djsaA

(Spot the old one out.)

(Chassez l'intrus.)

¼"kkls ySaFkzqlA½

(Sha-say lain-troos.)

a) euÒkou (agreeable) (agréable) ¼vÄzsvkCy½ (agray-able)

b)vPNk (kind) (gentil) ¼t©arh½ (jahng-tee)

c) cqjk (bad) (mauvais) ¼e¨os½ (mo-vay)

d) fouhr (polite) (poli) ¼i¨yh½ (po-lee)

Ans. (c) Mauvais is usually an adjective that modifies a noun and means bad, mean, wrong, etc. Mal means bad, ill-at-ease, immoral, etc., and can only be used as an adjective with copular (state-of-being) verbs such as être (to be) and se sentir (to feel). Il a de mauvais yeux. He has bad eyes (can't see).

20. ;g vko";d gS fd rqe ;g dke vkt "kke d¨ ________ A

(It's necessary that you ____ this work this evening.)

(Il faut que tu _____ ce travail ce soir.)

¼by Q¨ d R;q _____ l Fkzkok; l lqvkjA½

(eel fo k tyoo _____ suh thra-vaee suh soo-aar.)

a) dj¨xs (will do) (feras) ¼Qjk½ (fuh-rah)

b) dj¨ (do) (fasses) ¼vk Q¢½ (faas)

c) fd;k Fkk (did) (as fait) ¼vk Q¢½ (aa fay)

d) dj jgs g¨ (doing) (fais) ¼Q¢½ (fay)

Ans. (b) fasses is the subjonctif présent of verb 'faire' for second person singu lar.

21. ________ & i¨"kkd 300 ;qj¨ dh gSA

(______ – the dress costs 300 euros.)

(______ – la robe coûte 300 euros.)

¼ _____ &yk j¨c dwr Fkzqvk l© vj¨A½

(_____ – laa robe koot trwa-sahng uh-row.)

a) ;s i¨"kkd fdrus dh gS\ (How costs the dress?) (Comment coûte la robe?) ¼d¨e¨ dwr yk j¨c\½ (komo koot laa robe?)

b) ;s i¨"kkd किसकी gS \ (Who costs the dress?) (Qui coûte la robe?) ¼dh dwr yk j¨c\½ (kee koot laa robe?)

c) ;s D;k gS\ (What is this?) (Qu'est ce que c'est?) ¼dSl d lS\½ (kais kuh say?)

d) 300 ;qj¨ dk D;k gS\ (What costs 300 euros?) (Qu'est ce qui coûte 300 euros?) ¼dSl dh dwr Fkzqvk l¨a vj¨\½ (kais kee koot trwa sahng uh-row?)

Ans. (d) You use "Qu'est-ce qui..." if "qui" is the subject of the following sentence. And you use "qu'est-ce que..." if "que" is the direct object of the sentence. For example: Qu'est-ce que tu as fait?

22. ekjlsb ________ Ýkjl esa fLFkr gSA

(Marseille is situated in _____ of France.)

(Marseille se trouve au ______ de la France.)

¼ekjls;h l Fkzwo v¨ _____ n yk Ý©alA½

(Maar-Sayee suh troov o ______ duh laa France.)

a) mÙkj (north) (nord) ¼u©j½ (nor)

b) iwoZ (east) (est) ¼,sLr½ (aist)

c) nf{k.k (south) (sud) ¼L;qn½ (syood)

d) if"pe (west) (ouest) ¼m,sLr½ (oo-aist)

Ans. (c) Marseille is the prefecture of the French department of Bouches-du-Rhône and capital of the Provence-Alpes-Côte d'Azur region.

23. ;s i¨“kkd nwljh ls ______ gSA

(This dress is _____ than the other.)

(Cette robe est ______ que l’autre.)

¼lSr j¨c , _____ d y¨FkzA½

(Sait robe ay _____ kuh lotre.)

a) T;knk lqanj (more beautiful) (plus joli) ¼lyw t¨yh½ (ploo-jolee)

b) T;knk lqanj (more beautiful) (plus jolie) ¼lyw t¨yh½ (ploo-jolee)

c) lo¨ZÙke (best) (meilleur) ¼esb;j½ (may-ear)

d) lo¨ZÙke (best) (meilleure) ¼esb;j½ (may-ear)

Ans. (b) The French adverb plus has different pronunciations, depending on how it's used. Generally speaking, when plus has a positive meaning (e.g., more, extra, additional) it is pronounced [ploos]. When it is used as a negative adverb (meaning "no more"), it is usually pronounced [ploo].

24. _______ ÝSap gSA

(______ is French.)

(_____ est française.)

¼_____ , Ý©alSt+A½

(______ ay frahng-saiz.)

a) xkcjh;Sy lckrhuh (Gabrielle sabatini) (Gabrielle sabatini) ¼xkcjh;Sy lkckrhuh½ (Gaab-ree-ail Saa-baa-teenee)

b) ekVÊuk ghuthl (Martina Hingis) (Martina Hingis) ¼ekrÊuk buthl½ (Maar-teena in-jees)

c) eSjh iSlZ (Mary Peirce) (Mari Peirce) ¼ekjh iSlZ½ (Maa-ree Pair-suh)

d) LVsQh xzkQ (Steffi Graf) (Steffi Graf) ¼LrSQh ÄzkQ½ (Stai-fee Graaf)

Ans. (c) Mary Pierce is a retired tennis professional who represented France internationally in team compete-tions and the Olympics.

25. gekjs n¨Lr gkbrh ls gSaA os ________ gSaA

(Our friends are from Haïti. They are __________ .)

(Nos amis sont d'Haïti. Ils sont _____ .)

¼u¨ t+keÈ l¨a nkbrhA by l¨a _____ A½

(No zaami song daa-eeti . eel song _______ .)

a) gkbfrmvk (Haïtiois) (Haïtiois) ¼vkbrhmvk½ (aa-ee-tiwa)

b) gkbfrvu (Haitians) (Haïtiennes) ¼vkbfr;Su½ (aaee-tee-aine)

c) gkbfrvu (Haitians) (Haïtiens) ¼vkbfr;kj½ (aaee-tee-ang)

d) gkbfr;s (Haïtiais) (Haïtiaïs) ¼vkbfr,½ (aaee-tee-ay)

Ans. (c) Haitian French (French: français haïtien, Haitian Creole: fransè ayisyen) is the variety of French spoken in Haiti.... Haitian French is close to standard French.

26. ________ ÝSap ugÈ gSaA

(______ is not French.)

(______ n'est pas français.)

¼ _____ us ik Ý©alsA½

(_____ nay paa frahng-say.)

a) yk ekVÊu (La Martine) (La Martine) ¼yk ekrÊu½ (laa maar-tin)

b) c¨nySj (Baudelaire) (Baudelaire) ¼c¨nySj½ (bo-duh-laire)

c) VSuhlu (Tennyson) (Tennyson) ¼rSuhl¨a½ (tai-nee-song)

d) ojySu (Verlaine) (Verlaine) ¼oSjySu½ (vair-laine)

Ans. (c) Tennyson. 1809–92, English poet; poet laureate (1850–92). His poems include The Lady of Shalott (1832), Morte d'Arthur (1842).

27. 1841 esa foDVj º;qx¨ d¨ ________ esa pquk x;kA

(In 1841, Victor Hugo was elected at ______.)

(En 1841, Victor Hugo est élu à ______.)

¼v©a ehy mÃr l©a dSj¨ars vka] foDrj ;qx¨ , rsY;q vk _____A½ (ahng meel ooit sahng kai-rontay-ang, vik-tor ugo ay tailyoo aa _______.)

a) vkVZ v©j fyVjspj vdkneh (academy of arts & literature) (l'Académie des arts et des lettres) ¼ykdkneh nst+ vkj , ns ySFkz½ (Laa-kaa-dummy day zaar ay day lai-tre)

b) u;¨a dh vdkneh (academy of news) (l'Académie des neufs) ¼ykdkneh ns uQ½ (Laka-dummy day nuhf)

c) ÝSap vdkneh (French academy) (l'Académie française) ¼ykdkneh Ý©alSt½ (Laka-dummy frahng-saize)

d) vejhdu vdkneh (American academy) (l'Académie américaine) ¼ykdknseh vkesfjdSu½ (Laka-dummy aa-may-ree-kaine)

Ans. (c) In France, Hugo is renowned for his poetry collecti-ons, such as Les Contemplations (The Contem-plations) and La Légende des siècles (The Legend of the Ages).

28. dy] ek¡ Äj ij ________ A

(Tomorrow, mom _____ at home.)

(Demain, maman ______ à la maison.)

¼neka] eSe¨a _____ vk yk est+¨aA½

(duh mang, mai-mong ______ a laa mai-zong.)

a) vkjke djsaxh (are going to rest) (vas se reposer) ¼ok l ji¨t+s½ (vaa suh repo-zay)

b) vkjke djrh gS (is resting) (reposes) ¼ji¨t+½ (repoze)

c) vkjke djsaxh (will rest) (se reposera) ¼l ji¨t+jk½ (suh repo-zra)

d) vkjke djk Fkk (took rest) (a reposé) ¼vk ji¨t+s½ (aa repo-zay)

Ans. (c) French verb conjugation for reposer; Indicative; Present. je repose tu reposes il repose nous reposons vous reposez ils reposent ; Present perfect. j'ai repose.

**29. dy eqfj;y us D;k ________ **

(What _____ Muriel do, yesterday?)

(Qu'est-ce que Muriel _____ hier?)

¼dSld E;qjh;Sy _____ b;Sj\½

(kaisk myoo-riel ______ ee-air?)

a) fd;k Fkk (did) (a fait) ¼vk Q¢½ (aa fay)

b) fd;k Fkk (did) (as fait) ¼vk Q¢½ (aa fay)

c) djsxk (will do) (feras) ¼Qjk½ (fuh-raah)

d) djsxk (will do) (fera) ¼Qjk½ (fuh-raah)

Ans. (a) The present tense conjugation of faire is: Je fais (I do), Tu fais (You do, familiar), Il, elle fait (He, she does), Nous faisons (We do).

30. _______ xkM+h can gSA D;k ge _______ ys tk,¡

(______ car has run out of gas. Can we take _________ ?)

(______ voiture est en panne. Peut-on prendre ________?)

¼ _______ oqvkP;q , r¨a ikuA i r¨a iz©anz _____ \½

(_____vwa-tyoor ay tong paan, puh-tong prahng-dre ___ ?)

a) esjk] rsjk (my, your's) (mon, le tien) ¼e¨a] y fr;k¡½ (mong, luh tee-yang)

b) ;s] o¨ (This, that) (cette, celui-là) ¼lSr] सलुइ&yk½ (sait, suh-louis-laa)

c) esjh] rsjk (my, your's) (ma, le tien) ¼ek] y fr;k¡½ (maa, luh tee-yang)

d) esjh] vkidh (my, your's) (ma, la vôtre) ¼ek] yk o¨Fkz½ (Maa, laa vo-tre)

Ans. (d) To say that something belongs to "you all" or "you guys" in colloquial English, French speakers use votre (your) for both masculine and feminine nouns. For plural nouns, however, you use vos. Où est votre stylo ? (Where is your pen?) Est-ce que ceci est votre voiture ? (Is this your car?)

31. ;g E;q~ft+;e 'y ywoz' ls ________ ¼iqjkuk½ gSA

(This museum is _____ (old) than 'Le Louvre'.)

(Ce musée est ______ (ancient) que « le Louvre ».)

¼ls E;wt+s , _____ ¼v©afl;kj½ d y ywozA½

(suh myoo-zay ay _____ (ahng-see-yang) kuh luh loo-vre)

a) T;knk iqjkus (older) (plus anciens) ¼lyw t+©fl;ka½ (Ploo ahng-see-yang)

b) de iqjkuk (less older) (moins ancien) ¼ewvk t+©fl;kj½ (mwa-ahng-see-ya)

c) de iqjkus (less older) (moins anciennes) ¼ewvk t+©afu;Su½ (mwa-zahng-see-yeng)

d) d¢ ftruk iqjkuk (as old as) (aussi ancien) ¼v¨lh v¨afl;ka½ (o-see ahng-see-yang)

Ans. (d) "Ancien" in French can be used to mean "old" when it is placed AFTER a noun. Ce sont des bijoux anciens. These are ancient jewels. C'est une église ancienne.

32. ________ Qkby iwjh gSA

(______ file is complete.)

(_____ dossier est complet.)

¼ _____ n¨fl;s , d¨aiysA½

(______ do-see-ay ay kong-play.)

a) ;g (This) (ce) ¼l½ (suh)

b) ;g (This) (cet) ¼lSr½ (sait)

c) ;g (This) (cette) ¼lSr½ (sait)

d) ;s (These) (ces) ¼ls½ (say)

Ans. (a) Ce-masculin singular, – adjectif démonstratif

ce / cet *(m.) (this, that)*

cette *(f.) (this, that)*

ces *(pl.) (these, those)*

33. 'n ¶ykolZ v¨Q bfoy' fdl dfo dh fdrkc gS

(The flowers of evil is a work of which poet?)

("Les fleurs du mal" est l'oeuvre célèbre du quel poète?)

¼ßys फ्लर n~;q ekyß , yoz IsySÒz n dSy i¨,sr\½

(Lay fluh-re dyoo maal ay luh-vre say-laibre duh kail po-ait?)

a) c¨nySj (Baudelaire) (Baudelaire) ¼c¨nySj½ (Bo-duh-laire)

b) oSjySu (Verlaine) (Verlaine) ¼oSjySu½ (Vair-laine)

c) jSaec¨n (Rimbaud) (Rimbaud) ¼jSaec¨½ (Rang-bo)

d) ekykjes (Mallarmé) (Mallarmé) ¼ekykjes½ (Maa-laar-may)

Ans. (a) Charles Pierre Baudelaire was a French poet who also produced notable work as an essayist and art critic. His poems exhibit mastery in the handling of rhyme.

34. mldh n¨ cgusa gSaA ________ cgusa dys"knk;h gSaA

(He has two sisters. ______ sisters are troublesome.)

(Il a deux soeurs. ______ soeurs sont pénibles.)

¼by vk n ljA _____ lj l¨a isfuCyA½

(eel aa duh seur. ______ seur song pay-nee-ble.)

a) mldh (his) (ses) ¼ls½ (say)

b) og (The) (la) ¼yk½ (Laa)

c) mldh (her) (sa) ¼lk½ (saa)

d) ,d (one) (une) ¼;wu½ (yoon)

Ans. (a) Finally, ses means "his" or "her" and is used for both masculine and feminine nouns in the plural. Non, c'est son café ! (No, that's his/her coffee!)

35. lkjk us ________ xkM+h dh pkch [k¨ nhA

(Sarah lost the keys of ______ car.)

(Sarah a perdu le clé de _____ voiture.)

¼lkjk vk iSjn~;q y Dys n _____ oqvkP;qjA½

(Sarah aa pair-dyoo luh klay duh ______ vwa-choor.)

a) viuh (her) (sa) ¼lk½ (saa)

b) viuh (his) (son) ¼l¨a½ (song)

c) esjh (my) (mes) ¼es½ (Mai)

d) rqEgkjh (your) (ton) ¼r¨a½ (tong)

Ans. (a) Sa means "his" or "her" as well and is used for feminine nouns. Finally, ses means "his" or "her" and is used for both masculine and feminine nouns in the plural. Non, c'est son café ! (No, that's his/her coffee!)

36. gj lqcg] og lkr cts _______ gSA

(Every morning, he _____ at 7:00 AM.)

(Chaque matin, il ______ à sept heures.)

¼"kkd ekrka] by _____ vk lSr vjA½

(Shaak maa-tang, eel _____ aa sait err.)

a) rqEgsa txkrk (wakes you) (te levez) ¼r yos½ (tuh le-vay)

b) eq>s txkrk (wakes me up) (me lèvent) ¼e ySo½ (muh laiv)

c) eq>s txkrk (wakes me up) (me lève) ¼e ySo) (muh laiv)

d) txrk (wakes up) (se lève) ¼l ySo½ (suh laiv)

Ans. (d) For instance, to say "I am lifting," you would say "je lève." Likewise, "we will lift" is "nous lèverons."

37. og t¨ Òh i<+rk gS] mls ges"kk ________ tkrk gSA

(He ______ everything that he studies.)

(Il ______ toujours tout ce qu'il étudie.)

¼by _____ rqtqj rw l dhy ,R;qnhA½

(eel _____ too-joor too suh kil ay-tyoo-dee.)

a) ilan (likes) (aime) ¼,se½ (aim)

b) j[kuk (put) (met) ¼es½ (may)

c) Òwy (forgets) (oublie) ¼mCyh½ (oo-blee)

d) ihrk (drinks) (boit) ¼cqvk½ (bwa)

Ans. (c) The French verb oublier means "to forget." When you want to say "I forgot" in the past tense or "he is forgetting" in the present tense.

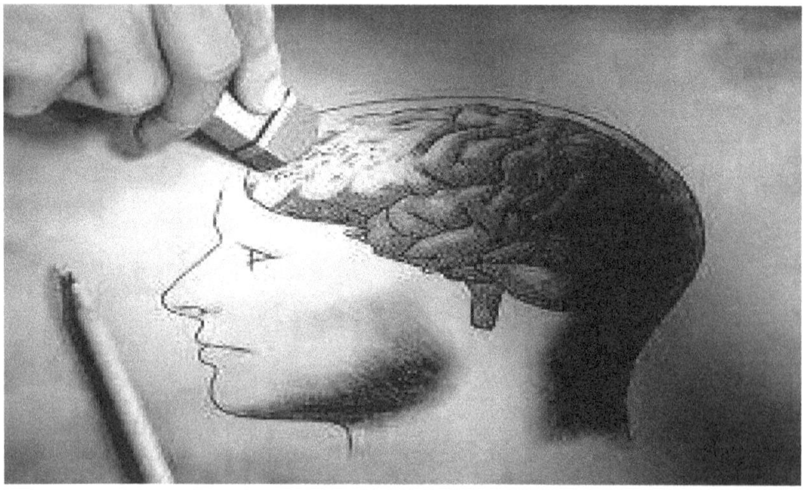

Hi,

I am happy to inform that I have released foreign language learning tutorials at Amazon Kindle free of cost as below:

French book: How can a Beginner be Expert in French Speaking, Reading & Writing through English & Hindi : https://www.amazon.in/dp/B0B5PQ7HR3/ref=sr_1_1?crid=3S1E92N9W6LSN&keywords=B0B5PQ7HR3&qid=1656924029&sprefix=b0b5pq7hr3+%2Caps%2C178&sr=8-1

French book: Introduction of France: Introduction to France: https://www.amazon.in/Introduction-France-Manish-Soni-ebook/dp/B09YPWKJ2L/ref=sr_1_1?crid=2I30KV0GOWM2D&keywords=B09YPWKJ2L&qid=1652609707&sprefix=b09ypwkj2l%2Caps%2C422&sr=8-1

French book: French Alphabets: Learn French Alphabets: https://www.amazon.in/French-Alphabets-Learn-ebook/dp/B09Z9NGJ41/ref=sr_1_1?crid=1WDO0VRAE3Q2Y&keywords=B09Z9NGJ41&qid=1652609937&sprefix=b09z9ngj41%2Caps%2C188&sr=8-1

French book: French Accent: Learn French Accent: https://www.amazon.in/French-Accent-Learn-ebook/dp/B09ZBHKXDL/ref=sr_1_1?crid=3VGU5120T0MEZ&keywords=B09ZBHKXDL&qid=1652609880&sprefix=b09zbhkxdl%2Caps%2C207&sr=8-1

French book: French Punctuation Marks: Punctuation Marks in French: https://www.amazon.in/French-Punctuation-Marks-ebook/dp/B09YZ793H1/ref=sr_1_1?crid=28LK31S5WELMR&keywords=B09YZ793H1&qid=1652609774&sprefix=b09yz793h1%2Caps%2C190&sr=8-1

French book: French pronunciation like a French native speaker: Learn French pronunciation from English and Hindi with Manish Soni Kindle Edition: https://www.amazon.in/French-pronunciation-like-native-speaker-ebook/dp/B09ZFDM9MM/ref=sr_1_1?crid=2KZUHXMUB6AC6&keywords=B09ZFDM9MM&qid=1652610007&sprefix=b09zfdm9mm%2Caps%2C233&sr=8-1

French book: French Number: Learn Numbers in French from English and Hindi with Pronunciation: https://www.amazon.in/ French-Number-Numbers-English-Pronunciation-ebook/dp/ B09ZNZD1HK/ref=sr_1_1?crid=2G0PKO41YAJE8&keywords=B09ZNZD1HK&qid=1652610062&sprefix=b09znzd1hk%2Caps%2C187&sr=8-1

French book: French Time: Learn Time telling in French language from English and Hindi: https://www.amazon.in/ French-Time-telling-language-English-ebook/dp/ B09ZQVGX7T/ref=sr_1_1?crid=ASZV6TEPN58Q&keywords=B09ZQVGX7T&qid=1652610113&sprefix=b09zqvgx7t%2Caps%2C181&sr=8-1

French book: Days, Months, Year and other related words in French: Calendar in French: https://www.amazon.in/Months-other-related-words-French-ebook/dp/B09Z3XVG27/ref=sr_ 1_ 1?crid=U763SL964KP9&keywords=B09Z3XVG27&qid=1652609825&sprefix=b09z3xvg27%2Caps%2C197&sr=8-1

French book: French Colours: How to learn Colours in French by English and Hindi: https://www.amazon.in/French-Colours-learn-English-Hindiebook/dp/B09ZSKL1H9/ref=sr_1_1?crid=14I8S6Z3COE72&keywords=B09ZSKL1H9&qid=1652610155&sprefix=b09zskl1h9%2Caps%2C183&sr=8-1

French book: French Quantity: Learn Quantity in French by English and Hindi Bilingual: https://www.amazon.in/French-Quantity-Learn-English-Bilingual-ebook/dp/B09ZVLL3SR/ref=sr_1_1?crid=2F82LT9MV2MAU&keywords=B09ZVLL3SR&qid=1652610253&sprefix=b09zvll3sr%2Caps%2C180&sr=8-1

French book: French Direction: Speak Directions in French like a Native French speaker by English and Hindi: https://www.amazon.in/French-Direction-Directions-speaker-English-ebook/dp/B0B12XGWM3/ref=sr_1_1?crid=1TUQQ4C5CTB7W&keywords=B0B12XGWM3&qid=1652610298&sprefix=b0b12xgwm3%2Caps%2C183&sr=8-1

French book: Human Body Parts in French: Speak body parts in French by English and Hindi like a Native speaker: https://www.amazon.in/Human-Body-Parts-French-English-ebook/dp/B0B121GJ5J/ref=sr_1_1?crid=36MMQKGY8XFXN&keywords=B0B121GJ5J&qid=1652610197&sprefix=b0b121gj5j%2Caps%2C183&sr=8-1

French book: French Clothes: Speak Clothes in French like a Native French speaker:https://www.amazon.in/French-Clothes-Speak-Native-speaker-ebook/dp/B0B15LMFFD/ref=sr_1_1?Crid=ERRWA1O8FOT2&keywords=B0B15LMFFD&qid=1652610345&sprefix=b0b15lmffd%2Caps%2C187&sr=8-1

French book: French Food: Speak Food items in French like a Native French speaker from English and Hindi: https://www.amazon.in/French-Food-Native-speaker-English-ebook/dp/B0B19WC7BD/ref=sr_1_1?crid=4HY6W6AE7NOD&keywords=B0B19WC7BD&qid=1652610397&sprefix=b0b19wc7bd%2Caps%2C542&sr=8-1

French book: French Fruits and Vegetables: Speak Fruits and Vegetables in French like a Native French speaker from English and Hindi: https://www.amazon.in/dp/B0B1BV5X2T/ref=sr_1_1?crid=24YHADZ9QSSH9&keywords=B0B1BV5X2T&qid=1652592398&s=digital-text&sprefix=b0b1bv5x2t%2Cdigital-text%2C390&sr=1-1

French book: French Health & Illness: Speak French Health & Illness words like a Native French speaker within 2 days: https://www.amazon.in/dp/B0B1H3R3TV/ref=sr_1_1?crid=Y80I2IRSSXJR&keywords=B0B1H3R3TV&qid=1652769911&s=digital-text&sprefix=b0b1h3r3tv%2Cdigital-text%2C433&sr=1-1

French book: French Jobs and Professions: Speak French Professions like a Native French speaker within two days: https://www.amazon.in/dp/B0B1MXZ4Z5/ref=sr_1_1?crid=2SRZM3A7RZ8PD&keywords=B0B1MXZ4Z5&qid=1652882717&s=digital-text&sprefix=b0b1mxz4z5%2Cdigital-text%2C397&sr=1-1

French book: French House: Learn House parts in French like a Native French speaker from English and Hindi: https://www.amazon.in/dp/B0B1QPXQ3T/ref=sr_1_1?keywords=B0B1QPXQ3T&qid=1652973513&s=digital-text&sr=1-1

French book: House Work: House work by French family members: https://www.amazon.in/dp/B0BDQNXWFW/ref=sr_1_1?crid=WIEKQAOT3NJF&keywords=B0BDQNXWFW&qid=1662777230&sprefix=b0bdqnxwfw%2Caps%2C207&sr=8-1

French book: French Nature: French Nature: Speak about French Nature like a Native French Speaker within two days: https://www.amazon.in/s?k=B0BDX79D52&crid=VRFPFZXBR2F1&sprefix=b0bdx79d52%2Caps%2C235&ref=nb_sb_noss

Dutch book: How can a beginner be expert in Dutch: How to learn Dutch from English and Hindi Kindle Edition: https://www.amazon.in/How-can-beginner-expert-Dutch-ebook/dp/B09Z8GW894/ref=sr_1_1?crid=21388RZY33UDL&keywords=B09Z8GW894&qid=1652610511&sprefix=b09z8gw894%2Caps%2C182&sr=8-1

Swedish book: How can a Beginner be Expert in Swedish: How to learn Swedish from English and Hindi Kindle Edition: https://www.amazon.in/How-can-Beginner-Expert-Swedish-ebook/dp/B09Z8G6W6T/ref=sr_1_1?crid=3I8DHRI5HABDJ&keywords=B09Z8G6W6T&qid=1652610455&sprefix=b09z8g6w6t%2Caps%2C221&sr=8-1

Interested professionals, teachers and students can read.

Printed book is as below:

French book: https://www.amazon.in/dp/B0B7S2MKSV?ref=myi_title_dp

Regards,
Manish Soni

9 789369 916474

Printed at Repro India Ltd.